MW00614588

101 Things®
To Do With
Popcorn

101 Things To Do With Popcorn

BY
CHRISTINA DYMOCK

GIBBS SMITH
TO ENRICH AND INSPIRE HUMANKIND

First Edition
16 15 14 13 12   5 4 3 2 1

Published by
Gibbs Smith
P.O. Box 667
Layton, Utah 84041

1.800.835.4993 orders
www.gibbs-smith.com

Printed and bound in Korea
Gibbs Smith books are printed on either recycled, 100% post-consumer
waste, FSC-certified papers or on paper produced from sustainable PEFC-
certified forest/controlled wood source. Learn more at www.pefc.org.

Library of Congress Cataloging-in-Publication Data
Dymock, Christina, 1978-
  101 things to do with popcorn / Christina Dymock. — 1st ed.
     p. cm.
  ISBN 978-1-4236-0689-5
1. Cooking (Popcorn) 2. Popcorn. 3. Cookbooks. I. Title.
II. Title: One hundred and one things to do with popcorn.
III. Title: One hundred one things to do with popcorn.
  TX814.5.P66D96 2012
  641.6'5677—dc23
                        2011027641

To my family.
I love you all more than words can say.

**More recipes and tips
at 101yum.com**

CONTENTS

Sweet Snacks

Kettle Corn 64 • Cookies and Cream 65 • Very Vanilla 66 • Pecan Pie 67 • Malted Milk Madness 68 • Caramel Corn 69 • Soft Caramel Corn 70 • Butter Nut Corn 71 • Toffee Corn 72 • Vanilla Pop 'n' Nuts 73 • Snickerdoodle 74 • Apple Pie a la Mode 75 • Cinnamon Sugar 76 • Peaches and Cream 77 • Summer Strawberry 78 • Blueberry Muffin 79 • Black Cherry Blitz 80 • Lemon Meringue 81 • Strawberries and Cream 82 • Strawberry Banana 83 • Island Pineapple 84 • Sour Lemon 85 • Kool Strawberry 86

Chocolate Popcorn

Almond Joy 88 • S'mores 89 • Gooey Goodness 90 • Chocolate Dream Pie 91 • Chocolate Drizzle 92 • Chocolate Pecan 93 • Peanut Butter Snackers 94 • Chocolate-Coated Brittle 95 • Candy Store 96 • French Cocoa 97 • Hot Cocoa 98 • Peanut Blossom 99 • Falling for Chocolate 100 • Milk Chocolate Hazelnut 101 • Banana Split with Fudge 102 • White Chocolate Caramel 103 • White Chocolate Macadamia Nut 104 • Salty Pecan 105

There's Popcorn in This?

Poppin' Muffins 108 • CinnaPop Cake 109 • Apri-Pop Slices 110 • Chocolate Muffins 111 • Popcorn Brownies 112 • Fudge Crumble Bars 113 • Banana-Pop Bread 114 • Rooster Snacks 115 • Chicken Tenders 116 • Chicken Sandwiches 117 • Grape Pitas 118 • Stuffed Peppers 119 • Swedish Meatballs 120 • Turkey Stuffing 121

HELPFUL HINTS

1. A regular-size bag of microwave popcorn makes 8 cups of popped popcorn. Most recipes in this book use 8 cups—or a multiple of 8 cups—of popcorn to make using microwave popcorn easy.

2. Two cups of popped popcorn is considered one serving.

3. Be sure to remove any unpopped kernels before you add seasoning or coat popcorn. In the world of popcorn, there is nothing worse than killing your teeth on an unpopped kernel. A quick way to remove these kernels is to place a wire cooling rack over a bowl of popcorn. Invert the bowl and rack and lightly jiggle, allowing the unpopped kernels to fall out of bowl.

4. Always store your popcorn in an airtight container *after* it has cooled and dried. If you seal it too soon, the moisture makes the popcorn go limp.

5. There are many recipes in this book that are wonderful for gifts, especially the chocolate popcorns.

6. Cellophane bags, with or without decorations, are wonderful packaging for popcorn gift giving. Add a tag and a little bit of ribbon and you have a treat for any occasion.

7. When using a paper bag of any sort, be sure to line it with a plastic bag or wax paper as the grease in the popcorn will soak through and stain the paper bag.

8. Mushroom popcorn works best for savory flavors. The shape tends to hold up under the liquid and lends itself to nontraditional popcorn flavors. You may need to order mushroom popcorn online if you can't find it at your favorite grocery store.

9. If you are working with a sticky popcorn, whether to make a bar or ball, coat your hands with a nonstick cooking spray. You may have to reapply before you finish. The spray will not change the flavor of the popcorn.

10. Always overestimate the size of your mixing bowl. It's better to have more than enough room in your bowl than too little.

11. When popcorn is used in a non-traditional recipe, such as muffins, brownies and etc., it adds a texture much like a nut. When the popcorn is ground to a powder it makes bread lighter. Finally, when added as a breading, as in Chicken Tenders (p. 116), it has much the same texture as bread crumbs. Don't be shy about trying popcorn in some of your own favorite recipes!

BALLS & BARS

TRADITIONAL POPCORN BALLS

I jar (7 ounces)	**marshmallow creme**
I teaspoon	**vanilla**
8 cups	**popped popcorn**

Place open jar of creme in microwave and cook at 50% power for I minute. Watch carefully so it doesn't bubble over.

In a large bowl, mix together the marshmallow creme and vanilla. Add popcorn and stir until well-coated. Grease your hands by rubbing with butter or spraying with nonstick cooking spray. Shape popcorn mixture into 8 balls. Place balls on a sheet of wax paper to set.

Wrap individually or store in an airtight container. Makes 8 servings.

SNOW BALLS

I jar (7 ounces)	**marshmallow creme**
I teaspoon	**coconut flavored extract**
I teaspoon	**vanilla**
8 cups	**popped popcorn**
2 cups	**shredded coconut**

Place open jar of creme in microwave and cook at 50% power for I minute. Watch carefully so it doesn't bubble over.

In a large bowl, mix together the marshmallow creme, coconut extract, and vanilla. Add popcorn and stir until well-coated. Grease your hands by rubbing with butter or spraying with nonstick cooking spray. Shape popcorn mixture into 8 balls. Roll balls in coconut and place on a sheet of wax paper to set.

Wrap individually or store in an airtight container. Makes 8 servings.

PEANUT BUTTER BALLS

I jar (7 ounces)	**marshmallow creme**
I teaspoon	**vanilla**
¼ cup	**peanut butter**
8 cups	**popped popcorn**
¾ cup	**peanut butter chips**

Place open jar of creme in microwave and cook at 50% power for I minute. Watch carefully so it doesn't bubble over.

In a large bowl, mix together the marshmallow creme, vanilla, and peanut butter. Add popcorn and peanut butter chips and stir until well-coated. Grease your hands by rubbing with butter or spraying with nonstick cooking spray. Shape popcorn mixture into 8 balls. Place balls on a sheet of wax paper to set.

Wrap individually or store in an airtight container. Makes 8 servings.

MARSHMALLOW BALLS

8 cups	**popped popcorn**
3 tablespoons	**butter or margarine**
2 cups	**mini marshmallows**

Place popcorn in a large bowl and set aside.

In a medium sauce pan, melt together the butter and marshmallows on low heat. Once the marshmallows have completely melted, pour the marshmallow mixture over popcorn and stir to coat. Grease your hands by rubbing with butter or spraying with nonstick cooking spray. Shape popcorn mixture into 8 balls. Place balls on wax paper to set.

Once set, about an hour, wrap individually or store in an airtight container. Makes 8 servings.

MMMM BALLS

1 jar (7 ounces)	**marshmallow creme**
1 teaspoon	**vanilla**
8 cups	**popped popcorn**
8	**Popsicle sticks**
2 cups	**mini M&M's**

Place open jar of creme in microwave and cook at 50% power for 1 minute. Watch carefully so it doesn't bubble over.

In a large bowl, mix together the marshmallow creme and vanilla. Add popcorn and stir until coated. Grease your hands by rubbing with butter or spraying with nonstick cooking spray. Shape popcorn mixture into 8 balls. Insert Popsicle sticks into balls and then roll balls in M&M's. Place balls on a sheet of wax paper to set.

Wrap individually with plastic wrap. Tie at base of ball with a ribbon to secure. Makes 8 servings.

VARIATION: Peanut MMMM Balls can be made by adding $\frac{1}{2}$ cup salted peanuts with the popcorn and rolling in Reece's Pieces.

BLUE RASPBERRY BALLS

I jar (7 ounces)	**marshmallow creme**
I tablespoon	**light corn syrup**
2 tablespoons	**dry blue raspberry gelatin mix**
8 cups	**popped popcorn**

In a small saucepan, melt the marshmallow creme, corn syrup, and gelatin. Gelatin can be a little grainy. Pour over popcorn and stir to coat. Grease your hands by rubbing with butter or spraying with nonstick cooking spray. Shape popcorn mixture into 8 balls. Place on a sheet of wax paper to set.

Wrap individually or store in an airtight container. Makes 8 servings.

STRAWBERRY BALLS

I jar (7 ounces)	**marshmallow creme**
I tablespoon	**dry strawberry gelatin mix**
8 cups	**popped popcorn**
I cup	**crushed graham crackers**

Place open jar of creme in microwave and cook at 50% power for I minute. Watch carefully so it doesn't bubble over.

In a large bowl, mix together the marshmallow creme and gelatin. Add popcorn and stir until well-coated. Grease your hands by rubbing with butter or spraying with nonstick cooking spray. Shape popcorn mixture into 8 balls. Roll in graham cracker crumbs. Place balls on a sheet of wax paper to set.

Wrap individually or store in an airtight container. Makes 8 servings.

PUMPKIN BALLS

1 jar (7 ounces)	**marshmallow creme**
1 teaspoon	**vanilla**
$1/4$ cup	**pumpkin quick bread mix**
8 cups	**popped popcorn**

Place open jar of creme in microwave and cook at 50% power for 1 minute. Watch carefully so it doesn't bubble over.

In a large bowl, mix together the marshmallow creme, vanilla, and bread mix. Add popcorn and stir until well-coated. Grease your hands by rubbing with butter or spraying with nonstick cooking spray. Shape popcorn mixture into 8 balls. Place balls on a sheet of wax paper to set.

Wrap individually or store in an airtight container. Makes 8 servings.

VARIATION: Banana bread mix or blueberry muffin mix can be used in place of the pumpkin bread mix. For a chocolate version, add $1/2$ cup semi-sweet chocolate chips with the popcorn.

OATMEAL BARS

2 cups	**popped popcorn**
3 $\frac{1}{2}$ cups	**old-fashioned rolled oats**
$\frac{1}{4}$ cup	**wheat germ**
1 cup	**shredded coconut**
$\frac{1}{2}$ cup	**raw sunflower seeds**
$\frac{1}{2}$ cup	**walnuts**
$\frac{3}{4}$ cup	**sugar**
$\frac{1}{4}$ cup	**butter or margarine,** melted

Preheat oven to 350 degrees.

Combine dry ingredients, then add butter and mix well. Press into a 9 x 13-inch pan and cook for 10 minutes or until edges are browned. While still warm, cut into bars. Allow to cool in the pan. Store in an airtight container. Makes 12 servings.

CHOCOLATE PRETZEL BARS

1 cup	**chocolate chips,** divided
1 cup	**corn syrup**
1/2 cup	**sugar**
8 cups	**popped popcorn**
1/2 cup	**broken pretzel rods**
1 cup	**Crispix or Chex cereal**

In a medium saucepan, melt 1/2 cup chocolate chips, corn syrup, and sugar over medium heat until combined; do not boil. Remove from heat.

In a large bowl, combine the popcorn, pretzels, cereal, and remaining chocolate chips. Pour melted chocolate mixture over popcorn mixture and stir to coat. Pour into a 9 x 9-inch pan and press down. Let set 4 hours. Cut into bars and serve. Store in an airtight container. Makes 9 servings.

O'PETER BARS

1 cup	**sugar**
1 cup	**light corn syrup**
1 cup	**peanut butter**
$^1/_2$ cup	**peanuts**
1 $^1/_2$ cups	**puffed rice cereal**
2 cups	**popped popcorn**
2 cups	**milk chocolate chips**

In a medium saucepan, melt the together the sugar, corn syrup, and peanut butter until sugar dissolves. Add peanuts, cereal, and popcorn. Spread into a 9 x 13-inch pan that has been prepared with nonstick cooking spray.

In a separate saucepan, melt chocolate chips over low heat. Spread over popcorn mixture and refrigerate until set. Makes 12 servings.

CARAMEL NUT BARS

16 cups	**popped popcorn**
2 cups	**peanuts**
1 $\frac{1}{2}$ cups	**milk chocolate chips**
1 tablespoon	**butter or margarine**
$\frac{3}{4}$ cup	**dark corn syrup**
$\frac{1}{4}$ teaspoon	**baking soda**

In an extra large bowl, mix together the popcorn, peanuts, and chocolate chips.

In a small saucepan, bring the butter and corn syrup to a boil over medium heat. Remove from heat and add baking soda, stirring until the color changes to a light brown. Pour over popcorn mixture and stir to coat. Press into a 9 x 13-inch pan that has been prepared with nonstick cooking spray. Let cool and then cut into bars. Makes 16 servings.

DOUBLE BERRY BARS

2 1/2 cups	**old-fashioned rolled oats**
1 1/2 cups	**flour**
2 cups	**popped popcorn**
3/4 cup	**sugar**
1/4 teaspoon	**ground cloves**
1/2 teaspoon	**baking powder**
1/4 teaspoon	**salt**
1 teaspoon	**vanilla**
1 cup	**butter or margarine**
1 cup	**raspberry preserves**
1/2 cup	**blueberry preserves**

Preheat oven to 375 degrees.

In a large bowl, mix together the oats, flour, popcorn, sugar, cloves, baking powder, salt, and vanilla. Cut butter into 1/4-inch cubes and drop into popcorn mixture. Use a hand mixer to cut in butter chunks until the dry ingredients look like a coarse meal mixture.

Press half the popcorn mixture into the bottom of a 9 x 13-inch greased pan. Bake 13–15 minutes.

When crust is finished baking, drop both preserves by spoonful over crust and spread together. Don't mix together; just make sure the crust is coated. Sprinkle the remaining crumb mixture over top. Return pan to oven and bake for 20–25 minutes more, or until the top is slightly brown. Cool completely before serving. Makes 12 servings.

P.B. AND J. BARS

3 cups	**popped popcorn**
1 1/2 cups	**puffed rice cereal**
1 cup	**sugar**
1/2 cup	**light corn syrup**
3/4 cup	**strawberry jam**
1/4 teaspoon	**baking soda**
2 cups	**peanut butter chips**
1 tablespoon	**butter or margarine**

In a large bowl, combine the popcorn and cereal; set aside.

In a medium saucepan, melt together the sugar, corn syrup, and jam over medium heat until the sugar dissolves. Remove from heat and add baking soda. Pour over popcorn mixture and stir to coat. Spread into a 9 x 13-inch pan that has been prepared with nonstick cooking spray.

In a small saucepan, melt peanut butter chips and butter over low heat. Spread over popcorn mixture and refrigerate until set. Makes 12 servings.

NATURE'S SWEET ENERGY BARS

16 cups	**popped popcorn**
3 tablespoons	**sunflower seeds**
1 cup	**unsalted peanuts**
1 cup	**raisins**
2 cups	**oatmeal**
1 cup	**peanut butter**
1/2 cup	**butter or margarine**
1 package (10 ounces)	**marshmallows**

In a large bowl, toss together the popcorn, sunflower seeds, peanuts, raisins, and oatmeal; set aside.

In a large saucepan, combine the peanut butter, butter, and marshmallows. Melt over low heat, stirring constantly. Pour peanut butter mixture over popcorn mixture and stir to coat. Press into a 9 x 13-inch pan. Cut into bars while still warm, then refrigerate until set. Wrap individually and store in fridge. Makes 12 servings.

PROTEIN POWER BARS

2 cups	**popped popcorn**
$^1\!/_2$ cup	**oatmeal**
$^1\!/_2$ cup	**orange-flavored protein powder**
$^1\!/_2$ cup	**walnuts**
$^1\!/_2$ cup	**dried cranberries**
$^1\!/_2$ cup	**white chocolate chips**
I cup	**light corn syrup**

Mix together dry ingredients and then add corn syrup. Spread into a
9 x 13-inch pan that has been prepared with nonstick cooking spray.
Press together. Refrigerate until set then cut into bars. Wrap in plastic
wrap or store in an airtight container. Makes 12 servings.

GRANOLA & TRAIL MIXES

NOT YOUR GRANDMA'S OATMEAL GRANOLA

6 cups	**popped popcorn**
3 1/2 cups	**old-fashioned rolled oats**
1/4 cup	**flour**
1/4 cup	**shredded coconut**
1/2 cup	**raw sunflower seeds**
1/2 cup	**roughly chopped walnuts**
3/4 cup	**sugar**
1/2 cup	**butter or margarine**
1/4 cup	**honey**
2 tablespoons	**corn syrup**

Preheat oven to 350 degrees.

In a large bowl, combine dry ingredients; set aside.

In a small microwave-safe bowl, stir together the butter, honey, and corn syrup and microwave on high for 30 seconds. Pour liquid over dry ingredients and stir to coat. Press into a 9 x 13-inch pan and bake 10 minutes, or until edges are browned. Break into small pieces while still warm. Makes 12 servings.

ARE YOU NUTS FOR GRANOLA?

6 cups	**popped popcorn**
3 $\frac{1}{2}$ cups	**old-fashioned rolled oats**
$\frac{1}{4}$ cup	**flour**
$\frac{1}{4}$ cup	**peanuts**
$\frac{1}{2}$ cup	**pecan pieces**
$\frac{1}{4}$ cup	**cashews**
$\frac{1}{2}$ cup	**walnut pieces**
$\frac{3}{4}$ cup	**sugar**
$\frac{3}{4}$ cup	**butter or margarine,** softened
$\frac{1}{4}$ cup	**honey**
3 tablespoons	**corn syrup**

Preheat oven to 350 degrees.

In a large bowl, combine dry ingredients; set aside.

In a small microwave-safe bowl, stir together the butter, honey, and corn syrup and microwave on high for 30 seconds. Pour liquid over dry ingredients and stir to coat. Press into a 9 x 13-inch pan and bake for 10 minutes, or until edges are browned. Break into small pieces while still warm. Makes 12 servings.

SALTY GRANOLA

6 cups	**popped popcorn**
3 ½ cups	**old-fashioned rolled oats**
¼ cup	**flour**
¼ cup	**pretzels,** broken into bite-size pieces
½ cup	**goldfish crackers**
¼ cup	**raw sunflower seeds**
½ cup	**peanuts**
¼ cup	**sugar**
¾ cup	**butter or margarine,** melted
2 tablespoons	**corn syrup**

Preheat oven to 350 degrees.

In a large bowl, combine dry ingredients; set aside.

In a small microwave-safe bowl, stir together the butter and corn syrup and microwave on high for 30 seconds. Pour liquid over dry ingredients and stir to coat. Press into a 9 x 13-inch pan and bake for 10 minutes, or until edges are browned. Break into small pieces while still warm. Makes 12 servings.

WASATCH HIKER'S GRANOLA

6 cups	**popped popcorn**
3 1/2 cups	**old-fashioned rolled oats**
1/4 cup	**flour**
1/4 cup	**shredded coconut**
1/2 cup	**peanuts**
1/2 cup	**M&M's**
1/4 cup	**raisins**
3/4 cup	**sugar**
3/4 cup	**butter or margarine**
1/2 cup	**honey**
3 tablespoons	**corn syrup**

Preheat oven to 350 degrees.

In a large bowl, combine dry ingredients; set aside.

In a small microwave-safe bowl, stir together the butter, honey, and corn syrup and microwave on high for 30 seconds. Pour liquid over dry ingredients and stir to coat. Press into a 9 x 13-inch pan and bake for 10 minutes, or until edges are browned. Break into small pieces while still warm. Makes 12 servings.

MOUNTAIN TRAILS

8 cups	**popped popcorn**
$\frac{1}{2}$ cup	**mini twisted pretzels**
$\frac{1}{2}$ cup	**raisins**
$\frac{1}{2}$ cup	**roasted peanuts**
$\frac{1}{2}$ cup	**M&M's**

In a large bowl, combine all ingredients using a wooden spoon. Divide into small bags for individual servings. Makes 8 servings.

FAMILY OF NUTS

8 cups	**popped popcorn**
I cup	**mixed nuts**
$^1/_2$ cup	**peanuts**
$^1/_2$ cup	**slivered almonds**
3 tablespoons	**butter or margarine,** melted
$^1/_2$ teaspoon	**pepper**

In a large bowl, combine the popcorn and nuts. Pour butter over popcorn mixture and stir to coat. Sprinkle with pepper. Makes 8 servings.

YOGURT RAISIN MIX

4 cups	**popped mushroom popcorn**
½ cup	**vanilla yogurt–covered raisins**
½ cup	**walnut halves**
¼ cup	**M&M's**
¼ cup	**dried cranberries**
½ cup	**MultiGrain Cheerios**

In a large bowl, mix together all ingredients. Divide into small bags for individual servings. Makes 6 servings.

TEDDY BEAR MIX

6 cups	**popped popcorn**
3 1/2 cups	**old-fashioned rolled oats**
1/4 cup	**flour**
1 cup	**chocolate teddy bear–shaped graham crackers**
1 cup	**honey teddy bear–shaped graham crackers**
3/4 cup	**sugar**
3/4 cup	**butter or margarine**
1/2 cup	**honey**
3 tablespoons	**corn syrup**

Preheat oven to 350 degrees.

In a large bowl, combine dry ingredients; set aside.

In a small microwave-safe bowl, stir together the butter, honey, and corn syrup and microwave for 30 seconds. Pour liquid over dry ingredients and stir to coat. Press into a 9 x 13-inch pan and bake for 10 minutes, or until edges are browned. Break into small clusters while still warm. Makes 12 servings.

SLEEPOVER MIX

2 tablespoons	**dry lime gelatin mix**
½ cup	**light corn syrup**
2 tablespoons	**sugar**
8 cups	**popped popcorn**
¼ cup	**Skittles**
¼ cup	**gummy bears**
¼ cup	**licorice bites**

In a small saucepan, melt together the gelatin, corn syrup, and sugar over medium heat. Pour over popcorn and stir to coat. Spread popcorn on a baking sheet and refrigerate for about 1 hour, or until set. Once hard, break into small clusters.

In a large bowl, combine popcorn pieces and candy. Makes 6 servings.

APPLE CINNAMON MIX

4 cups	**popped popcorn**
I cup	**chopped dried apples**
2 cups	**Wheat Chex cereal**
3 tablespoons	**butter or margarine,** melted
2 tablespoons	**sugar**
I tablespoon	**dark corn syrup**
I teaspoon	**cinnamon**

In a large bowl, mix together the popcorn, apples, and cereal; set aside.

In a small microwave-safe bowl, combine butter, sugar, corn syrup, and cinnamon; microwave for I minute. Pour over popcorn mixture. Spread on a baking sheet and let cool about 5 minutes. Store in an airtight container. Makes 6 servings.

BREAKFAST ON THE RUN

8 cups	**popped popcorn**
4 cups	**Rice Chex**
4 cups	**Wheaties**
1 cup	**slivered almonds**
1 cup	**raisins or dried cranberries**
1 ½ cups	**sugar**
1 ½ cups	**light corn syrup**
1 cup	**butter or margarine**

In a large bowl, mix together the popcorn, cereals, almonds, and dried fruit; set aside.

In a medium saucepan, bring the sugar, corn syrup, and butter to a boil. Pour over dry ingredients and stir to coat. Spread over wax paper to dry and store in an airtight container. Makes 16 servings.

MIX IT UP!

4 cups	**popped popcorn**
1 cup	**Rice Chex**
1 cup	**Corn Chex**
1 cup	**pretzel twists**
1 cup	**bite-size Ritz crackers**
3 tablespoons	**butter or margarine,** melted
1 tablespoon	**Worcestershire sauce**
$^3/_4$ teaspoon	**seasoned salt**
$^1/_4$ teaspoon	**garlic powder**
$^1/_4$ teaspoon	**onion powder**

In a large bowl, combine the popcorn, cereals, pretzels, and crackers; set aside.

In a small bowl, combine the butter, Worcestershire sauce, seasoned salt, garlic powder, and onion powder. Pour over popcorn mixture and stir to coat. Makes 12 servings.

COWBOY MIX

2 cups	**Rice Chex**
2 cups	**popped popcorn**
I cup	**pretzel twists**
I cup	**Cheez-its crackers**
3 tablespoons	**butter or margarine,** melted
2 tablespoons	**ranch dressing mix**

In a large bowl, combine the cereal, popcorn, pretzels, and crackers;
set aside.

In a small bowl, combine the butter and dressing mix. Pour over
popcorn mixture and stir until evenly coated. Spread on a baking sheet
and let cool about 5 minutes. Store in an airtight container. Makes
8 servings.

DORM ROOM

3 tablespoons   **butter or margarine,** melted
1 package (3 ounces)   **chicken-flavored Ramen noodles,** broken into nickel-size pieces
8 cups   **popped popcorn**

In a large frying pan, melt butter over medium heat. Add broken noodles and stir for 3 minutes. Add the popcorn and stir for 2 minutes. Sprinkle seasoning packet over noodles and popcorn. Transfer mixture to a large bowl and cool slightly before serving. Makes 6 servings.

SAVORY
POPCORN

STOVETOP POPCORN

| 3 tablespoons | **vegetable oil** |
| 1/3 cup | **popcorn kernels** |

In a medium to large pot, heat the oil over medium heat for 2 minutes. Add popcorn to oil and cover with lid. If you do not use a lid, the kernels may fly out and burn you. Shake the pot back and forth or side to side to keep the kernels from burning. It takes about 5 minutes. Once the popcorn starts to pop, tip the lid to vent the steam. When half the kernels are popped you can remove the pan from the heat; make sure the lid is still tipped. Makes approximately 10 cups of popped popcorn.

VARIATION: Make cheesy popcorn by coating popped popcorn with 3 tablespoons melted butter and stirring in 1 package (1.5 ounces) dry cheese sauce powder.

PARMESAN

3 tablespoons	**butter or margarine,** melted
1 tablespoon	**grated Parmesan cheese**
$1/2$ teaspoon	**dried parsley**
$1/4$ teaspoon	**paprika**
$1/4$ teaspoon	**garlic powder**
	Dash of salt
8 cups	**popped popcorn**

In a small bowl, combine all ingredients except popcorn. Pour liquid over popcorn in a large bowl and toss to coat. Serve immediately. Makes 4 servings.

30-SECOND GOURMET

3 tablespoons	**butter or margarine,** melted
1 tablespoon	**Mrs. Dash**
10 cups	**popped popcorn**

In a small bowl, stir together the butter and Mrs. Dash seasoning. Pour over popcorn in a large bowl and stir to coat. Store in an airtight container. Makes 5 servings.

VARIATION: Use 1 tablespoon dry ranch dressing mix instead of Mrs. Dash to make ranch popcorn.

SOME LIKE IT HOT

¼ teaspoon	**minced dried onion**
⅛ teaspoon	**salt**
⅛ teaspoon	**crushed red pepper**
¼ teaspoon	**Italian seasoning**
⅛ teaspoon	**ground cumin**
5 tablespoons	**butter or margarine,** melted
16 cups	**popped popcorn**

In a small bowl, combine first five ingredients. Add butter and stir well. Pour mixture over popcorn in a large bowl and stir to coat. Makes 8 servings.

A TASTE OF THE ORIENT

3 tablespoons	**butter or margarine,** melted
I teaspoon	**stir-fry seasoning mix**
8 cups	**popped popcorn**
I cup	**chow mein noodles**

In a small bowl, stir together the butter and seasoning mix. Pour over popcorn and noodles in a large bowl and stir to coat. Serve warm. Makes 4 servings.

SUPERB SNACK

1/2 teaspoon	**minced dried onion**
1/2 teaspoon	**parsley**
1/4 teaspoon	**garlic powder**
1/2 teaspoon	**Italian seasoning**
1/4 teaspoon	**sugar**
3 tablespoons	**butter or margarine,** melted
8 cups	**popped popcorn**

In a small mixing bowl, combine all ingredients except popcorn. Pour over popcorn in a large bowl and stir to coat. Makes 4 servings.

LEANING TOWER

$\frac{1}{4}$ cup	**butter or margarine,** melted
$\frac{1}{2}$ teaspoon	**seasoned salt**
$\frac{1}{2}$ teaspoon	**dried basil**
8 cups	**popped popcorn**

In a small bowl, stir together the butter, seasoned salt, and basil. Pour over popcorn in a large bowl and stir to coat. Makes 8 servings.

GYRO GOODNESS

1 teaspoon	**steak-flavored grill seasoning**
1/8 teaspoon	**chili powder**
1/4 teaspoon	**cumin**
1/4 teaspoon	**coriander**
1/8 teaspoon	**oregano**
	Pinch of cinnamon
6 tablespoons	**butter or margarine,** melted
16 cups	**popped popcorn**
1/2 cup	**crumbled feta cheese**

In a small bowl, combine all ingredients except popcorn and cheese. Pour over popcorn in a large bowl and stir to coat. Add cheese and stir. Makes 8 servings.

GOOD THYME

3 tablespoons	**butter or margarine,** melted
1/4 teaspoon	**instant beef bouillon granules**
1/8 teaspoon	**ground thyme**
1/4 teaspoon	**onion powder**
1/8 teaspoon	**ground sage**
8 cups	**popped popcorn**

In a small bowl, mix together the butter and bouillon; stir until granules dissolve. Add remaining ingredients except popcorn. Pour over popcorn in a large bowl and stir to coat. Makes 4 servings.

CHEESE AND CHIVE

2 tablespoons	**butter or margarine,** melted
8 cups	**popped popcorn**
½ cup	**grated Parmesan cheese**
I teaspoon	**dried chives**

In a large bowl, pour butter over popcorn and stir to coat. Sprinkle cheese and chives over top and stir to coat. Store in an airtight container. Makes 4 servings.

OOO LA LA

1 teaspoon	**sugar**
$1/4$ teaspoon	**paprika**
$1/8$ teaspoon	**dry mustard**
$1/4$ teaspoon	**salt**
	Dash of onion powder
8 cups	**popped popcorn**

In a small bowl, combine all ingredients except popcorn. Pour mixture over popcorn in a large bowl and stir to coat. Makes 4 servings.

SASSY AND SAVORY

I teaspoon	**minced dried onion**
I teaspoon	**dried parsley**
$1/4$ teaspoon	**garlic salt**
$1/8$ teaspoon	**pepper**
3 tablespoons	**butter or margarine,** melted
8 cups	**popped popcorn**

In a small bowl, combine all ingredients except popcorn. Pour over popcorn in a large bowl and stir to coat. Makes 4 servings.

ITALIAN DELIGHT

¼ teaspoon	**dried cilantro**
¼ teaspoon	**sugar**
	Pinch of pepper
	Pinch of garlic powder
2 tablespoons	**butter or margarine,** melted
8 cups	**popped popcorn**
2 teaspoons	**grated Parmesan cheese**

In a small bowl, combine cilantro, sugar, pepper, garlic powder, and butter. Pour over popcorn in a large bowl and stir to coat. Sprinkle popcorn with cheese. Makes 4 servings.

FIRE GRILLED

¼ teaspoon	**salt**
¼ teaspoon	**pepper**
⅛ teaspoon	**red pepper flakes**
1 teaspoon	**A1 Steak Sauce**
2 tablespoons	**butter or margarine,** melted
8 cups	**popped popcorn**

In a small bowl, combine all ingredients except popcorn. Pour mixture over popcorn in a large bowl and stir to coat. Makes 4 servings.

CAESAR CORN

½ teaspoon	**grated lemon peel**
¼ teaspoon	**ground oregano**
	Dash of pepper
	Pinch of minced garlic
1 teaspoon	**grated Parmesan cheese**
3 tablespoons	**butter or margarine,** melted
8 cups	**popped popcorn**

In a small bowl, combine all ingredients except popcorn. Pour over popcorn in a large bowl and stir to coat. Makes 4 servings.

HONEY MUSTARD

3 tablespoons	**butter or margarine,** melted
I teaspoon	**honey mustard glaze seasoning mix**
8 cups	**popped popcorn**

In a small bowl, stir together the butter and seasoning mix. Pour over popcorn in a large bowl and stir to coat. Serve warm. Makes 4 servings.

SWEET SNACKS

KETTLE CORN

3 tablespoons	**vegetable oil**
$^1/_3$ cup	**popcorn kernels**
2 tablespoons	**sugar**
$^1/_3$ teaspoon	**salt**

Place oil in a large pot with lid. Make sure there is enough oil to cover the bottom of the pot. Add the popcorn, sugar, and salt and cover. Shake the pot back and forth to make sure the popcorn does not burn. It will take about 5 minutes for the popcorn to start popping. Once the popping becomes infrequent you can remove the pan from the heat. Makes 5 servings.

COOKIES AND CREAM

8 cups	**popped popcorn**
I cup	**crushed Oreo cookies**
³/₄ cup	**light corn syrup**
2 tablespoons	**instant vanilla pudding mix**
I tablespoon	**sugar**
¹/₄ teaspoon	**baking soda**

In a large mixing bowl, combine popcorn and cookies; set aside.

In a small saucepan, combine the corn syrup, pudding mix, sugar, and baking soda. Melt together over medium heat until sugar dissolves and mixture becomes thin; do not boil. Pour over popcorn mixture and stir to coat. Spread on a baking sheet to cool. Store in an airtight container. Makes 4 servings.

VERY VANILLA

¹/₂ cup	**light corn syrup**
2 tablespoons	**instant vanilla pudding mix**
I tablespoon	**sugar**
¹/₄ teaspoon	**baking soda**
8 cups	**popped popcorn**

In a small saucepan, combine the corn syrup, pudding mix, sugar, and baking soda. Melt together over medium heat until sugar dissolves and mixture becomes thin; do not boil. Pour over popcorn in a large bowl and stir to coat. Makes 4 servings.

PECAN PIE

8 cups	**popped popcorn**
I cup	**pecan halves,** roughly chopped
$1/4$ cup	**corn syrup**
$1/2$ cup	**brown sugar**
I tablespoon	**butter or margarine**
$1/4$ teaspoon	**baking soda**

In a large bowl, mix together the popcorn and pecans; set aside.

In a small saucepan, bring the corn syrup, brown sugar, and butter to a boil over medium heat. Once sugar dissolves, remove from heat and add baking soda. Pour over popcorn mixture and stir to coat. Spread on wax paper to cool. Store in an airtight container. Makes 4 servings.

MALTED MILK MADNESS

8 cups	**popped popcorn**
I cup	**coarsely chopped chocolate coated malt balls**
1/3 cup	**light corn syrup**
2 tablespoons	**malt**
1/4 teaspoon	**baking soda**

In a large bowl, mix together popcorn and malt balls; set aside.

In a small saucepan, bring the corn syrup and malt to a boil over medium heat. Remove from heat and add baking soda. Pour over popcorn mixture and stir to coat. Spread on wax paper or a baking sheet to cool. Makes 6 servings.

VARIATION: Use strawberry or peanut butter flavored malted milk balls in place of chocolate-coated ones.

CARAMEL CORN

¼ cup	**brown sugar**
¼ cup	**dark corn syrup**
¼ cup	**cream**
1 tablespoon	**butter or margarine**
1 teaspoon	**vanilla**
8 cups	**popped mushroom popcorn**

In a small heavy saucepan, bring the sugar and corn syrup to a boil over medium heat. Slowly add the cream and then add the butter and stir until melted. Bring to 220 degrees on a candy thermometer, stirring frequently. It will take about 15 minutes. Remove from heat and add vanilla. Allow to cool for 2 minutes before pouring over popcorn in a large bowl. Stir to coat and then spread on a large baking sheet that has been prepared with nonstick cooking spray; let set in the refrigerator for about 30 minutes. Store in an airtight container. Makes 8 servings.

SOFT CARAMEL CORN

2¼ cups	**brown sugar**
1 can (14 ounces)	**sweetened condensed milk**
1 cup	**light corn syrup**
½ cup	**butter or margarine**
	Pinch of salt
16 cups	**popped popcorn**

In a medium saucepan, over medium heat, cook all ingredients except popcorn, stirring constantly, until a candy thermometer reads 235 degrees. It will take about 15–17 minutes. Remove from heat and pour over popcorn in a large bowl. Stir to coat. Makes 8 servings.

BUTTER NUT CORN

1 package	**butter-flavor microwave popcorn**
¹/₂ cup	**brown sugar**
3 tablespoons	**light corn syrup**
2 tablespoons	**butter or margarine**
1 teaspoon	**butter nut flavoring,** or nut flavoring, of choice
¹/₂ cup	**coarsely chopped pecans**

Pop popcorn according to package directions and empty into a large mixing bowl; set aside.

In a small microwave-safe bowl, combine the brown sugar, corn syrup, and butter. Microwave on high for 1 minute. Stir until the brown sugar dissolves and add the butter nut flavoring. Pour over the popcorn and stir to coat. Spread the popcorn on wax paper. Sprinkle with pecans. Allow to cool before serving. Makes 8 servings.

TOFFEE CORN

8 cups	**popped popcorn**
1 cup	**sugar**
2 tablespoons	**dark corn syrup**
2 tablespoons	**butter or margarine**
1/2 cup	**water**
1 tablespoon	**vanilla**

Place popcorn in a large bowl and set aside.

In a medium saucepan, cook sugar, syrup, butter, and water on high until it comes to a boil. Reduce heat to medium and cook for 10 minutes. Remove from heat and add vanilla. Pour over popcorn and stir to coat. Spread on wax paper to cool. Store in an airtight container. Makes 4 servings.

VANILLA POP 'N' NUTS

8 cups	**popped popcorn**
I cup	**pecan halves**
8 tablespoons	**water**
I cup	**sugar**
I teaspoon	**vanilla**

Lightly prepare a baking sheet with nonstick cooking spray and set aside.

In a large bowl, mix popcorn and nuts; set aside.

In a small saucepan, bring the water and sugar to a boil over high heat, then lower the heat to medium and cook until the mixture turns golden brown and registers 300 degrees on a candy thermometer. This will take about 20 minutes. Remove from heat and add vanilla. Pour over popcorn mixture and stir to coat. Spread on the baking sheet to cool. Makes 4 servings.

SNICKERDOODLE

I teaspoon	**cinnamon**
¼ cup	**sugar**
I tablespoon	**butter or margarine**
½ cup	**corn syrup**
¼ teaspoon	**baking soda**
8 cups	**popped popcorn**

Lightly prepare a baking sheet with nonstick cooking spray and set aside.

In a small saucepan, bring the cinnamon, sugar, butter, and corn syrup to a boil over medium heat. Boil I minute. Add baking soda and stir well. Pour over popcorn in a large bowl and stir to coat. Spread on the baking sheet to cool. Makes 4 servings.

APPLE PIE A LA MODE

8 cups	**popped popcorn**
1/2 cup	**chopped dried apple pieces**
1/2 cup	**light corn syrup**
2 tablespoons	**instant vanilla pudding mix**
1 tablespoon	**sugar**
1/2 teaspoon	**cinnamon**
1/4 teaspoon	**baking soda**

In a large bowl, combine the popcorn and apple pieces; set aside.

In a small saucepan, combine the corn syrup, pudding mix, sugar, and cinnamon over medium heat until sugar dissolves and mixture becomes thin; do not boil. Remove from heat and add baking soda. Pour over popcorn mixture and stir to coat. Spread on a baking sheet to cool. Allow to set for about 1 hour. Store in an airtight container. Makes 4 servings.

CINNAMON SUGAR

3 tablespoons	**sugar**
1/2 teaspoon	**cinnamon**
1/4 cup	**butter or margarine,** melted
8 cups	**popped popcorn**

In a small bowl, combine the sugar and cinnamon and set aside. Pour melted butter over popcorn in a large bowl and stir to coat. Sprinkle sugar mixture over popcorn and stir to coat. Makes 4 servings.

PEACHES AND CREAM

¹/₂ cup	**marshmallow creme**
2 tablespoons	**light corn syrup**
2¹/₂ tablespoons	**dry peach gelatin mix**
8 cups	**popped popcorn**

In a small saucepan, melt together the marshmallow creme, corn syrup, and gelatin. Pour over popcorn in a large bowl and stir to coat. Spread onto wax paper to cool and set. Store in an airtight container. Makes 4 servings.

SUMMER STRAWBERRY

¼ cup	**dry strawberry gelatin mix**
½ cup	**light corn syrup**
¼ cup	**sugar**
8 cups	**popped popcorn**

In a medium saucepan, combine the gelatin, corn syrup, and sugar and cook to a rolling boil. Pour over popcorn in a large bowl. Stir to coat. Spread popcorn onto a baking sheet and allow to cool and set. Break into small clusters to serve. Makes 4 servings.

BLUEBERRY MUFFIN

3 tablespoons	**butter or margarine**
2 tablespoons	**dry blueberry muffin mix**
8 cups	**popped popcorn**

In a small microwave-safe bowl, melt the butter in microwave and stir in muffin mix. Pour over popcorn in a large bowl and stir to coat. Spread on wax paper to cool. Makes 4 servings.

BLACK CHERRY BLITZ

¹/₂ cup	**light corn syrup**
1 envelope (0.14 ounces)	**black cherry Kool-Aid**
2 tablespoons	**sugar**
¹/₄ teaspoon	**baking soda**
8 cups	**popped popcorn**

In a saucepan, bring the corn syrup, Kool-Aid, and sugar to a boil over medium heat. Remove from heat and add baking soda. Pour over popcorn in a large bowl and stir to coat. Spread on wax paper or a baking sheet to cool. Makes 4 servings.

LEMON MERINGUE

¹/₂ cup	**light corn syrup**
2 tablespoons	**sugar**
2 tablespoons	**instant vanilla pudding mix**
1 teaspoon	**lemonade drink mix**
¹/₄ teaspoon	**baking soda**
8 cups	**popped popcorn**

In a small saucepan, bring the corn syrup and sugar to a boil over medium heat. Remove from heat and stir in pudding mix and lemonade mix. Once incorporated, add baking soda and stir. Pour over popcorn in a large bowl and stir to coat. Spread on wax paper or a baking sheet to cool. Makes 4 servings.

STRAWBERRIES AND CREAM

¹/₂ cup	**light corn syrup**
2 tablespoons	**Nesquik Strawberry Drink Mix**
2 tablespoons	**sugar**
¹/₄ teaspoon	**baking soda**
8 cups	**popped popcorn**

In a small saucepan, bring the corn syrup, drink mix, and sugar to a boil over medium heat bring. Remove from heat and add baking soda. Pour over popcorn in a large bowl and stir to coat. Spread on wax paper or a baking sheet to cool. Makes 4 servings.

STRAWBERRY BANANA

$^1/_2$ cup	**light corn syrup**
2 tablespoons	**dry strawberry-banana gelatin mix**
1 tablespoon	**sugar**
$^1/_4$ teaspoon	**baking soda**
8 cups	**popped popcorn**

In a small saucepan, combine the corn syrup, gelatin, and sugar over medium heat until sugar dissolves and mixture becomes thin; do not boil. Remove from heat and add baking soda. Pour over popcorn in a large bowl and stir to coat. Spread on a baking sheet to cool. Store in an airtight container. Makes 4 servings.

VARIATION: Mix $^1/_2$ cup banana chips or dried strawberries with the popcorn before making the coating.

ISLAND PINEAPPLE

8 cups	**popped popcorn**
1/2 cup	**dried tropical fruit of your choice,** optional
1/2 cup	**light corn syrup**
2 tablespoons	**dry Island Pineapple gelatin mix**
1 tablespoon	**sugar**
1/4 teaspoon	**baking soda**

In a large mixing bowl, combine the popcorn and dried fruit; set aside.

In a small saucepan, combine the corn syrup, gelatin, and sugar over medium heat until sugar dissolves and mixture becomes thin; do not boil. Remove from heat and add baking soda. Pour over popcorn in a large bowl and stir to coat. Spread on a baking sheet to cool. Store in an airtight container. Makes 4 servings.

SOUR LEMON

¹/₂ cup	**light corn syrup**
I envelope (0.14 ounces)	**pink lemonade Kool-Aid**
2 tablespoons	**sugar**
8 cups	**popped popcorn**

In a small saucepan, bring the corn syrup, Kool-Aid, and sugar to a boil over medium heat. Pour over popcorn in a large bowl and stir to coat. Spread on wax paper to cool. Makes 4 servings.

KOOL STRAWBERRY

¹/₂ cup	**light corn syrup**
1 envelope (0.14 ounces)	**strawberry Kool-Aid**
3 tablespoons	**sugar**
¹/₄ teaspoon	**baking soda**
8 cups	**popped popcorn**

In a small saucepan, bring the corn syrup, Kool-Aid, and sugar to a boil over medium heat. Remove from heat and add baking soda. Pour over popcorn in a large bowl and stir to coat. Spread on wax paper or a baking sheet to cool. Makes 4 servings.

CHOCOLATE POPCORN

ALMOND JOY

1 ½ cups	**marshmallow creme**
2 tablespoons	**light corn syrup**
1 teaspoon	**almond extract**
8 cups	**popped popcorn**
2 cups	**shredded coconut**
1 cup	**slivered almonds**
1 ½ cups	**semisweet chocolate chips**

In a small saucepan, melt together the marshmallow creme and corn syrup over medium heat. Remove from heat and stir in almond extract. Pour marshmallow mixture over popcorn in an extra-large bowl and stir to coat. Add coconut and almonds; stir again. Spread mixture on a large baking sheet. Set aside to cool.

In a small microwave-safe bowl, heat chocolate chips in microwave for 1 minute at 50% power; stir. Continue to cook at 50% power, stirring at 30-second intervals, until smooth. Drizzle over popcorn. Refrigerate popcorn about 30 minutes to set. Store in an airtight container. Makes 6 servings.

S'MORES

30	**large marshmallows**
1 ½ tablespoons	**butter or margarine**
8 cups	**popped popcorn**
1 ½ cups	**milk chocolate chips**
1 cup	**honey teddy bear–shaped graham crackers**

In a large saucepan, melt the marshmallows and butter over medium heat. Pour over popcorn in a large bowl and stir to coat. Add chocolate chips and graham crackers and stir until evenly incorporated. Spread on a large baking sheet and refrigerate to set. If needed, break into smaller pieces to serve. Store in an airtight container. Makes 6 servings.

GOOEY GOODNESS

16 cups	**popped popcorn**
2 cups	**peanuts**
1 cup	**dark corn syrup**
1 tablespoon	**butter or margarine**
$1/4$ teaspoon	**baking soda**
$1 1/2$ cups	**milk chocolate chips**

In an extra-large bowl, mix together the popcorn and peanuts; set aside.

In a small saucepan, bring the corn syrup and butter to a boil over medium heat. Remove from heat and add baking soda. Pour over popcorn and stir to coat. Spread on wax paper to cool.

In a small microwave-safe bowl, heat chocolate chips in microwave for 1 minute on 50% power; stir. Microwave at 30-second intervals until chocolate is smooth. Do not over heat. Drizzle chocolate over popcorn. Allow to cool then break into smaller pieces to serve. Makes 10 servings.

CHOCOLATE DREAM PIE

¹/₂ cup	**light corn syrup**
2 tablespoons	**instant chocolate pudding mix**
I tablespoon	**sugar**
¹/₄ teaspoon	**baking soda**
8 cups	**popped popcorn**
I cup	**chocolate teddy bear–shaped graham crackers**

In a small saucepan, combine the corn syrup, pudding mix, and sugar. Melt together over medium heat until sugar dissolves and mixture becomes thin; do not boil. Remove from heat and add baking soda.

Pour chocolate mixture over popcorn in a large bowl and stir to coat. Incorporate graham crackers. Spread on a baking sheet and let set about I hour. If needed, break into smaller pieces before serving. Store in an airtight container. Makes 6 servings.

CHOCOLATE DRIZZLE

$\frac{1}{2}$ cup	**packed brown sugar**
4 tablespoons	**butter or margarine**
2 tablespoons	**light corn syrup**
$\frac{1}{4}$ teaspoon	**baking soda**
8 cups	**popped popcorn** (a salted microwave variety is delicious with the chocolate)
$\frac{1}{3}$ cup	**white chocolate chips**

In a small saucepan, melt together the brown sugar, butter, and corn syrup over medium heat. Remove from heat and add baking soda. Pour over popcorn in a large bowl and stir to coat. Spread on a baking sheet and let cool for 10–15 minutes.

In a small microwave-safe bowl, microwave chocolate chips at 50% power for 1 minute. Stir chips and cook again for 30 seconds; stir. Continue cooking for 30-second intervals until chips are melted and runny. Drizzle white chocolate over cooled popcorn. Place baking sheet in the refrigerator until chocolate sets. Break into clusters and store at room temperature in an airtight container. Makes 4 servings.

CHOCOLATE PECAN

8 cups	**popped popcorn** (a salted microwave popcorn is delicious in this recipe)
I cup	**pecan halves**
2 cups	**milk chocolate chips**
I cup	**white chocolate chips**

In a large bowl, combine the popcorn and pecans; set aside.

In a medium microwave-safe bowl, heat milk chocolate chips in microwave at 50% power for I minute; stir. Continue to microwave at 30 second intervals until chocolate is smooth. Pour chocolate over popcorn and nuts; stir to coat. Spread mixture on a baking sheet to cool.

Melt the white chocolate chips in microwave in the same manner as the milk chocolate chips. Drizzle over popcorn mixture; stir to coat.

Place popcorn in refrigerator to set. Once set, break into small clusters to serve. Store in an airtight container. Makes 6 servings.

PEANUT BUTTER SNACKERS

8 cups	**popped popcorn**
I cup	**salted peanuts**
I ½ cups	**peanut butter chips**
I cup	**milk chocolate chips**

In an extra-large bowl, combine the popcorn and nuts, being careful to remove any unpopped popcorn kernels.

In a small saucepan, melt the peanut butter chips over low heat. Pour over popcorn mixture and stir to coat. Spread on a baking sheet covered in wax paper.

Melt chocolate chips in the same manner as the peanut butter chips. Drizzle over popcorn mixture. Place in refrigerator for 30 minutes to set. Break into small pieces to serve. Store in an airtight container. Makes 4 servings.

CHOCOLATE-COATED BRITTLE

8 tablespoons	**water**
1 cup	**sugar**
16 cups	**popped popcorn**
1 bar (7 ounces)	**semisweet chocolate,** chopped

Lightly prepare a baking sheet with nonstick cooking spray and set aside.

In a small saucepan, bring water and sugar to a boil over high heat, then lower the heat to medium. Cook until the mixture turns golden brown and registers 300 degrees on a candy thermometer, about 5–10 minutes. Pour over popcorn in a large bowl and stir to coat. Spread popcorn on wax paper to cool. Once cooled, break into chunks.

In a small saucepan over low heat, melt the chocolate. Dip popcorn chunks into chocolate to cover half way. Place on wax paper to set. Makes 10 servings.

CANDY STORE

8 cups	**popped popcorn**
1 ½ cups	**milk chocolate chips**
1 teaspoon	**shortening**
½ cup	**mini Reese's Pieces**
½ cup	**mini M&M's**

Spread popcorn on a sheet of wax paper.

In a medium saucepan, melt together the chocolate chips and shortening over low heat. Drizzle over popcorn. Before chocolate sets, sprinkle with candies. Once set, break into small pieces for serving. Makes 6 servings.

FRENCH COCOA

3 tablespoons	**butter or margarine**
2 tablespoons	**French vanilla hot chocolate mix**
8 cups	**popped popcorn**

In a small microwave-safe bowl, melt the butter in the microwave. Add hot chocolate mix and stir. Pour chocolate mixture over popcorn in a large bowl and stir to coat. Makes 4 servings.

HOT COCOA

3 tablespoons	**butter or margarine**
2 tablespoons	**hot chocolate mix**
$\frac{1}{2}$ cup	**light corn syrup**
8 cups	**popped popcorn**
$\frac{1}{2}$ cup	**mini marshmallows**
$\frac{1}{4}$ cup	**crushed mint candy cane**

In a small saucepan, melt together the butter, hot chocolate mix, and corn syrup over medium heat.

In a large bowl, combine popcorn and marshmallows. Pour chocolate mixture over popcorn and stir to coat. Spread on waxed paper and sprinkle with crushed candy. Store in an airtight container. Makes 4 servings.

PEANUT BLOSSOM

2 tablespoons	**butter or margarine**
2 teaspoons	**peanut butter cookie mix**
8 cups	**popped popcorn**
1 $\frac{1}{2}$ cups	**semisweet chocolate chips**
3 teaspoons	**shortening**

In a small microwave-safe bowl, melt the butter in the microwave and add cookie mix. Pour over popcorn in a large bowl and stir to coat; set aside.

In a small saucepan, melt together the chocolate chips and shortening over low heat. Pour over popcorn and stir to coat. Spread on wax paper to cool. Store in an airtight container. Makes 4 servings.

FALLING FOR CHOCOLATE

2 tablespoons	**butter or margarine**
1 ½ teaspoons	**pumpkin quick bread mix**
8 cups	**popped popcorn**
1 ½ cups	**milk chocolate chips**
3 teaspoons	**shortening**

In a small microwave-safe bowl, melt the butter in microwave and add to bread mix. Pour over popcorn in a large bowl and stir to coat; set aside.

In a small saucepan, melt together the chocolate chips and shortening over low heat. Pour over popcorn and stir to coat. Spread on wax paper to cool. Store in an airtight container. Makes 4 servings.

MILK CHOCOLATE HAZELNUT

8 cups	**popped popcorn**
1/2 cup	**chopped hazelnuts**
1 1/2 cups	**milk chocolate chips**
3 teaspoons	**shortening**
2 tablespoons	**hazelnut-flavored**
	coffee creamer

Combine popcorn and hazelnuts in a large bowl; set aside.

In a small saucepan, melt together the chocolate chips and shortening over low heat.

Pour chocolate mixture over popcorn and nuts; stir to coat. Spread on wax paper to cool. Before chocolate hardens, sprinkle with creamer. Store in an airtight container. Makes 4 servings.

VARIATION: For an amaretto-cherry flavor, substitute 1/2 cup dried cherries for the hazelnuts and use amaretto-flavored creamer instead of hazelnut-flavored creamer.

BANANA SPLIT WITH FUDGE

2 tablespoons	**butter or margarine**
1 ½ teaspoons	**banana quick bread mix**
8 cups	**popped popcorn**
1 cup	**semisweet chocolate chips**
3 teaspoons	**shortening**

In a small microwave-safe bowl, melt the butter in microwave and add to bread mix. Pour over popcorn in a large bowl and stir to coat; set aside.

In a small saucepan, melt together the chocolate chips and shortening over low heat. Pour over popcorn and stir to coat. Spread on wax paper to cool. Store in an airtight container. Makes 4 servings.

WHITE CHOCOLATE CARAMEL

1 bag	**butter-flavored microwave popcorn**
$\frac{1}{2}$ cup	**brownie mix**
$\frac{3}{4}$ cup	**white chocolate chips**
$\frac{1}{2}$ cup	**caramel ice cream topping**

Pop the popcorn according to package directions. While it's still warm, dump it into a large bowl, being careful to remove any unpopped kernels, and sprinkle with brownie mix (the butter should help the brownie mix stick, but you will have some collect in the bottom of the bowl.)

In a small microwave-safe bowl, melt the white chocolate at 50% power for 1 minute and then stir. Continue melting at 50% power for 30-second intervals until the chocolate is smooth and runny.

Heat the caramel for 1 minute in the microwave. Pour the chocolate over the popcorn, immediately followed by the caramel. Stir to coat.

Cover a baking sheet with wax paper. Spread popcorn over wax paper and put in the refrigerator until set. Break into pieces then store in an airtight container. Makes 4 servings.

WHITE CHOCOLATE MACADAMIA NUT

8 cups	**popped popcorn**
I cup	**macadamia nuts,**
	coarsely chopped
I ½ cups	**white chocolate chips**
I ½ teaspoons	**shortening**

In a large bowl, mix together the popcorn and nuts; set aside.

In a small saucepan, melt together the white chocolate and shortening over low heat. Pour chocolate over popcorn mixture and stir to coat. Spread on wax paper to cool. Store in an airtight container. Makes 6 servings.

SALTY PECAN

8 cups	**popped popcorn**
1 cup	**pecan halves**
1 1/2 cups	**white chocolate chips**
1 1/2 teaspoons	**shortening**
1/2 teaspoon	**salt**

In a large bowl, combine the popcorn and nuts; set aside.

In a small saucepan, melt together the white chocolate and shortening over low heat. Pour chocolate over popcorn mixture and stir to coat. Spread on wax paper and sprinkle with salt; cool to set. Makes 4 servings.

THERE'S
POPCORN
IN THIS?

POPPIN' MUFFINS

2 cups	**flour**
2 cups	**popped popcorn,** chopped
4 teaspoons	**baking powder**
$^1/_2$ teaspoon	**apple pie spice**
$^1/_8$ teaspoon	**salt**
$^2/_3$ cup	**brown sugar**
$^1/_4$ cup	**chopped walnuts**
4 tablespoons	**butter or margarine,** melted
2	**eggs**
$^3/_4$ cup	**milk**
I teaspoon	**vanilla**
	Brown sugar

Preheat oven to 400 degrees. Line a 12-cup muffin tin with paper liners.

In a large bowl, stir together the flour, popcorn, baking powder, apple pie spice, salt, brown sugar, and nuts.

In a small bowl, stir together the butter, eggs, milk, and vanilla. Stir the liquid into the flour mixture. The batter should be lumpy. Fill muffin cups $^2/_3$ full and sprinkle with brown sugar. Bake 15 minutes, or until a toothpick inserted in the center comes out clean. Cool on a wire rack. Makes 12 servings.

CINNAPOP CAKE

½ cup	**butter or margarine**
½ cup	**butter-flavored shortening**
1 ¼ cups	**sugar**
2	**eggs**
1 teaspoon	**vanilla nut flavoring,** or vanilla
1 ¾ cups	**flour**
1 cup	**popped popcorn,** pulsed in food processor until a powder
1 teaspoon	**baking soda**
1 teaspoon	**baking powder**
1 cup	**sour cream**

Crumb topping:

2 tablespoons	**sugar**
½ teaspoon	**cinnamon**
¼ teaspoon	**nutmeg**
¼ cup	**chopped walnuts**
¼ cup	**chopped butter-flavored popped popcorn**

Whipped cream

Preheat oven to 350 degrees.

In a large bowl, combine the butter, shortening, sugar, eggs, and flavoring. Add flour, popcorn, baking soda, baking powder, and sour cream; mix well. Pour into a 9 x 13-inch cake pan.

In a small bowl, combine the sugar, cinnamon, nutmeg, walnuts, and popcorn. Sprinkle over cake batter and bake for 45–50 minutes, or until a toothpick inserted in the center comes out clean. Run a knife around edges of pan and allow to cool. Serve topped with whipped cream. Makes 12 servings.

APRI-POP SLICES

¹/₂ cup	**dried apricots,** chopped
1	**red delicious apple,** cored and grated
1 cup	**shredded coconut**
2 cups	**popped popcorn,** chopped into small pieces
²/₃ cup	**apple juice**
1 tablespoon	**butter or margarine,** softened

Preheat oven to 375 degrees.

In a large mixing bowl, combine all the ingredients. Press mixture into an 8 x 8-inch pan that has been prepared with nonstick cooking spray. Bake for 35–40 minutes, or until lightly browned. Cut into slices while warm. Allow to cool in the pan. Makes 8 servings.

CHOCOLATE MUFFINS

½ cup	**butter or margarine,** melted
9 tablespoons	**unsweetened cocoa powder**
¼ cup	**milk**
2 tablespoons	**canola oil**
1 cup	**sugar**
1	**egg**
1 cup	**buttermilk**
2 teaspoons	**vanilla**
2½ cups	**flour**
1 teaspoon	**baking soda**
2 cups	**popped popcorn,** chopped
1 cup	**chopped pecans**
1 cup	**milk chocolate chips**

Preheat oven to 375 degrees. Line a 12-cup muffin tin with paper liners.

In a large bowl, combine all the ingredients and stir until just blended. Fill muffin cups ⅔ full. Bake 15–20 minutes, or until a toothpick inserted in the center comes out clean. Remove from pan and cool on a wire rack. Makes 12 servings.

POPCORN BROWNIES

¹/₂ cup	**canola oil**
1 ¹/₄ cups	**brown sugar**
2	**eggs**
1 teaspoon	**vanilla**
1 tablespoon	**butter or margarine**
5 bars (1 ounce each)	**semisweet chocolate,** chopped
1 cup	**flour**
1 ¹/₂ cups	**popped popcorn,** chopped
4 tablespoons	**unsweetened cocoa powder**
³/₄ cup	**chopped walnuts**
¹/₄ cup	**milk chocolate chips**

Preheat oven to 350 degrees. Prepare a 9 x 9-inch pan with nonstick cooking spray; set aside.

In a large bowl, beat together the oil, brown sugar, eggs, and vanilla; set aside.

In a small saucepan, melt butter and chocolate together over low heat. Add to oil mixture and beat until well combined. Add flour, popcorn, cocoa, walnuts, and chocolate chips. Pour into the pan and bake 30–35 minutes. Allow to cool in the pan before cutting. Makes 9 servings.

FUDGE CRUMBLE BARS

Crust:

½ cup	**butter or margarine,** room temperature
1	**egg,** slightly beaten
1 teaspoon	**vanilla**
1 cup	**brown sugar**
1 cup	**flour**
1 ½ cups	**chopped popped popcorn**
½ teaspoon	**baking soda**
½ teaspoon	**salt**
1 cup	**quick oats**

Fudge Filling:

1 cup	**milk chocolate chips**
1 ¼ cups	**sweetened condensed milk**
1 tablespoon	**butter or margarine**
1 teaspoon	**vanilla**

Preheat oven to 350 degrees.

In a large bowl, cream together the butter, egg, vanilla, and brown sugar. Add flour, popcorn, baking soda, salt, and oats; blend well. Grease the bottom of a 9 x 9-inch pan. Spread ⅔ of the crust mixture over the bottom of the pan, reserving the remaining mixture.

In a small saucepan, melt the chocolate chips, condensed milk, and butter over low heat, stirring often to keep the chocolate from burning. When melted, add vanilla and spread over crust in pan. Drop rounded teaspoonfuls of reserved crust mixture over the fudge filling. (There will be holes.) Bake 25–30 minutes or until center is set. Cool before cutting. Makes 9 servings.

BANANA-POP BREAD

1 ¾ cups	**flour**
2 cups	**popped popcorn,** chopped
2 teaspoons	**baking soda**
1 ½ teaspoons	**ground ginger**
1 ½ cups	**rolled oats**
¼ cup	**brown sugar**
⅓ cup	**butter or margarine**
⅔ cup	**light corn syrup**
1	**egg**
3	**over-ripe bananas,** mashed
	Powdered sugar

Preheat oven to 325 degrees. Grease and flour a large bread pan; set aside.

In a large bowl, combine the flour, popcorn, baking soda, ginger, and oats; set aside.

In a medium saucepan, melt the brown sugar, butter, and corn syrup over medium heat until the sugar dissolves; do not boil. Pour over flour mixture and stir. Add egg and bananas. Pour into prepared pan and bake 60–70 minutes, or until a toothpick inserted in the center comes out clean. Allow to cool in the pan then remove and dust with powdered sugar. Makes 8 servings.

ROOSTER SNACKS

1 package (3 ounces)	**cream cheese**
1 can (5 ounces)	**chicken,** drained
1/3 cup	**dried cranberries**
1/4 cup	**almonds**
1/4 tablespoon	**dried parsley**
1/4 tablespoon	**dried basil**
1/2 teaspoon	**Worcestershire sauce**
1 clove	**garlic,** minced
1 cup	**popped popcorn,** ground in food processor

In a food processor, combine the cream cheese, chicken, cranberries, almonds, parsley, basil, Worcestershire sauce, and garlic until smooth. Make chicken into tablespoon-size balls. Roll the balls in the popcorn and serve. Store in the refrigerator. Makes 4 servings.

CHICKEN TENDERS

I bag	**Orville Redenbacher's Garlic Herb and Olive Oil Gourmet Popping Corn**
I teaspoon	**Mrs. Dash tomato and garlic seasoning**
I	**egg**
2 tablespoons	**milk**
I pound	**chicken tenders**
⅓ cup	**flour**

Preheat oven to 350 degrees.

Pop popcorn according to package directions. Place in a food processor, being careful to remove any unpopped kernels, and pulse until popcorn becomes a powder.

In a shallow dish, combine popcorn and Mrs. Dash. In a second dish, beat together the egg and milk, and sift flour into a third dish.

Rinse the chicken and coat in flour, dip in egg mixture, and then roll in popcorn mixture. Place on a greased baking sheet and bake 15–20 minutes, or until chicken is cooked through. Makes 6 servings.

CHICKEN SANDWICHES

1 package (8 ounces)	**cream cheese**
$^1/_2$ cup	**Miracle Whip**
2 tablespoons	**spicy brown mustard**
1 can (12.5 ounces)	**chicken,** drained
$^1/_2$	**red bell pepper,** chopped
1 stalk	**celery,** chopped
1	**medium carrot,** grated
1 cup	**popped popcorn,** chopped
$^1/_4$ teaspoon	**coarse-ground pepper**
	bread or pitas
	alfalfa sprouts
	tomato slices
	lettuce
	cucumber slices

In a large bowl, combine the cream cheese, Miracle Whip, mustard, chicken, bell pepper, celery, carrot, popcorn, and pepper. Spread onto bread or in pitas. Garnish with vegetables, as desired. Makes 4 servings.

GRAPE PITAS

1 can (12.5 ounces)	**chicken,** drained
3 tablespoons	**Miracle Whip**
1 cup	**popped popcorn**
$\frac{1}{2}$ teaspoon	**seasoned salt**
$\frac{1}{2}$	**red apple,** chopped
1 stalk	**celery,** chopped
$\frac{1}{4}$ cup	**green grape halves**
$\frac{1}{8}$ cup	**salted cashews**
1	**green onion,** chopped
	pitas
	alfalfa sprouts
	cucumber slices

In a food processor, combine the chicken, Miracle Whip, popcorn, and seasoned salt until well mixed.

In a medium bowl, combine the chicken mixture with the apple, celery, grapes, cashews, and onion; chill for 30 minutes. Spoon into pitas and garnish with sprouts and cucumbers. Makes 4 servings.

STUFFED PEPPERS

1 tablespoon plus 1 teaspoon	**butter or margarine,** divided
1 cup	**uncooked rice**
2 cups	**chicken broth**
1	**carrot**
1	**zucchini**
1 stalk	**celery**
8 cups	**popped garden herb and olive oil microwave popcorn,** coarsely chopped
4	**green bell peppers**

Preheat oven to 350 degrees.

In a small frying pan, melt 1 teaspoon butter over medium heat. Add rice and cook until rice begins to brown. Add chicken broth and cover. Reduce heat to medium-low and cook for 20 minutes, or until the liquid is absorbed and rice is tender.

Meanwhile, finely chop the carrot, zucchini, and celery.

In a large frying pan, saute the vegetables in remaining butter until cooked through. Incorporate rice mixture and popcorn.

Cut off tops of green peppers and core; stuff with rice and vegetable mixture. Place on a baking sheet and bake for 30 minutes. Makes 4 servings.

SWEDISH MEATBALLS

2 cups	**popped popcorn**
¹/₂ cup	**skim milk**
I pound	**ground beef**
I	**egg**
I teaspoon	**onion powder**
¹/₂ teaspoon	**dried basil**
I teaspoon	**salt**
¹/₄ teaspoon	**allspice**
2 tablespoons	**extra virgin olive oil**
I cup	**beef or vegetable stock**

In a food processor, pulse popcorn until a powder.

In a medium bowl, combine the milk and popcorn; let sit for a few minutes. Add the ground beef, egg, onion powder, basil, salt, and allspice. Knead together with your hands until mixed and then form into 16 balls.

In a large frying pan, warm the oil over low heat. Add meatballs and cook until brown on all sides and cooked through. Pour in stock and loosen browned bits on the bottom of the pan with a wooden spoon. Simmer about 10–15 minutes. Makes 4 servings.

TURKEY STUFFING

1 box (3.6 ounces)	**turkey stuffing**
1 $^1/_2$ cups	**water**
$^1/_4$ cup	**butter or margarine**
8 cups	**popped popcorn**

In a large microwave-safe dish, combine the stuffing, water, and butter. Microwave 5 minutes. Add popcorn and stir together. Microwave 1 minute more. Serve warm. Makes 6 servings.

NOTES

NOTES

NOTES

NOTES

NOTES

METRIC CONVERSION CHART

Volume Measurements		Weight Measurements		Temperature Conversion	
U.S.	Metric	U.S.	Metric	Fahrenheit	Celsius
1 teaspoon	5 ml	1/2 ounce	15 g	250	120
1 tablespoon	15 ml	1 ounce	30 g	300	150
1/4 cup	60 ml	3 ounces	90 g	325	160
1/3 cup	75 ml	4 ounces	115 g	350	180
1/2 cup	125 ml	8 ounces	225 g	375	190
2/3 cup	150 ml	12 ounces	350 g	400	200
3/4 cup	175 ml	1 pound	450 g	425	220
1 cup	250 ml	2 1/4 pounds	1 kg	450	230